abba Father

What's next, Papa?

AYO AJANI

Tyrannus House

Unless otherwise indicated, all Scripture quotations in this book are from the King James Version (KJV) of the Bible.

Scripture quotations marked TPT are taken from The Passion Translation of the Bible.

Scripture quotations marked NIV are taken from the New International Version of the Bible.

Scripture quotations marked AMPC are taken from the Amplified Bible, Classic Edition.

Scripture quotations marked AMP are taken from the Amplified Bible.

Scripture quotations marked TLB are taken from The Living Bible.

Scripture quotations marked MSG are taken from The Message Bible.

Scripture quotations marked NCV are taken from the New Century Version of the Bible.

First published in Nigeria in 2019 by Tyrannus House

ISBN: 978-978-959-737-6

Tyrannus House Limited
www.tyrannushouse.org
hello@tyrannushouse.org

Printed in the United States of America
Cover Page & Book Design by Steve Dubs

Contents

Preface

Dear Reader,

As you will soon find out, contained in the pages of this book are some of the most revolutionary insights from the Bible.
I say that not because I authored the book, but because I read it just like you are about to do and every time I did, I was blessed afresh.

It is an unusual book because of the depth and breadth of its message; something that rarely exists in our readings today. It is deep enough to edify you and broad enough to be balanced.

In the pages of this book, I expounded your rights as a son and your responsibilities as a servant, two legs upon which the full measure of the stature of Christ rests.

My prayer is that as you read this book, your heart will be established in the truth of God's Word, and His grace will become evident in your life.

Ayo Ajani
November 2019

abba Father

What's next,
Papa?

"So don't you see that we don't owe this old do-it-yourself life one red cent. There's nothing in it for us, nothing at all. The best thing to do is give it a decent burial and get on with your new life.

God's Spirit beckons. There are things to do and places to go! This resurrection life you received from God is not a timid, grave-tending life.

It's adventurously expectant, greeting God with a childlike

"What's Next, Papa?"

God's Spirit touches our spirits and confirms who we really are.

We know who he is, and we know who we are: Father and children.

And we know we are going to get what's coming to us - an unbelievable inheritance!

We go through exactly what Christ goes through. If we go through the hard times with him, then we're certainly going to go through the good times with him!"

THE APOSTLE PAUL,
THE LETTER TO THE ROMANS, CHAPTER 8, VERSES 12-16
MESSAGE BIBLE

Abba Father

It was very late at night.

It was almost midnight before they set out of the upper room. A few hours before, He had stooped to wash their feet, served them supper and said some of the scariest things they had ever heard in their lives.

Quietly, they make their way through the streets of Jerusalem. The streets are still very alive. It's Passover, one of Israel's three annual festivals. Passover pilgrims were everywhere. They set up camp on any empty lot available. The streets were littered with groups and families camped around fires to stay warm. Many others were asleep, wearied from the busy activities of the day. These band of men from the upper room passed through the lower pool unnoticed by these pilgrims, exiting the city through the fountain gate.

Right ahead of them as they journeyed towards the Kidron Valley was Mount Olives. The beautiful Garden of Gethsemane sits at the foot of the mountain. It's a familiar place as they often met there. Thirteen men left the upper room, but one had slipped away quietly as they made their way through the streets. The lure of material gains was stronger than the love from the One who had washed his feet. He would soon negotiate His Creator for the same price as a slave.

No one could have imagined the significance of the moments ahead. The only thing that probably gave it away was the eerie stillness that enveloped the night. Even nature knew something was about to happen. Man's future stood at the mercy of tonight's events.

Both Adams had a garden. What Eden was to Adam, Gethsemane was to the Last Adam. Will the Last Adam fail? He's the last. There's no hope of redemption after Him.

The Garden of Gethsemane was as still as the night. It was one of the most beautiful places you ever saw. The birds chirped away as the winds blew gently, with the bigger birds hooting loudly every now and then. The Last Adam and His eleven made their way through the grove of twisted olive trees, carefully avoiding the large chunks of rocks that cluttered the ground. It was going to be a long dark night.

Leaving the others in a cave by the edge of the Garden, He thrust further with three of His friends, two brothers and a third one. By now, He was visibly disturbed and heavily burdened by the thoughts of what lay ahead of Him. He turned back and said to them,

"My heart is overwhelmed and crushed with grief. It feels as though I'm dying. Stay here and keep watch with me."
(Matthew 26:38, TPT)

For a minute, I am reminded of the classic portrait of Jesus in the garden. Looking so in charge and unruffled. Dressed in an exquisite white flowing robe, kneeling beside a huge rock with his hands lifted towards heaven in peaceful prayer.

This is so far from the truth. He was filled with grief, anguish and sorrow. It was a man going through an agonising ordeal we see depicted by the Gospels. The writer of Hebrews would later describe it this way,

"During the days of Jesus' life on earth, He offered up prayers and petitions with loud cries and tears to the one who could save him from death."
(Hebrews 5:7 NIV)

A more accurate picture would have been of a solitary figure, flat on the ground, writhing and groaning in agony.

Intermittently, He looks up into heaven as though He were expecting a relief package. With tears streaming down His cheeks, He bends over pounding his fists over and over into the hard earth. His eyes are bloodshot. His golden hair looked more like brown as his sweat had made mud of the dusty ground soiling his hair. In the agony of prayer, His sweat pores broke and started leaking blood. The glistening white robe he wore was now patterned with drops of blood, sweat and mud.

This is Jesus. My Jesus. Your Jesus. The lowly man of Galilee. The man of sorrows and well acquainted with grief.

In the backdrop were three men snoring heavily: Peter, James and his brother John. They couldn't be bothered. Don't blame them; it had been a long twenty-four hours plus.

The Apostle Mark records His prayers thus:
"Abba, Father, all things are possible unto thee; take away this cup from me: nevertheless not what I will, but what thou wilt."
(Mark 14:36)

At a cursory glance, this sounds like a pious prayer. It sounds like what you hear the priests say at the altar in the big cathedrals, with the organs playing soul-stirring hymns as a soundtrack. But no!

This was a cry. It was the most intense prayer ever uttered by a man. In such contradictory situations, He shouted, "Abba, Father!"

To give context, Jesus wasn't shying away from the cross like many presume. Not at all. That's precisely why He came. All through His three-year ministry, He was always speaking about His death. He knew He was going to be crucified. And yes, He wanted to die.

As Jesus looked into heaven, you and I were his vision. He dreamed of the day when we would be where He is. His final prayer was about you. His final pain was for you. His final passion was you.

Never had He felt so alone. Only He could do what had to be done. No angel could do it. A man couldn't do it. No man had the purity to destroy sin's claim. No force on earth could face the force of evil and win— except God.

He begged to be delivered from the cup of suffering that He was about to drink. Standing at the edge of death's canyon, Jesus peered into the dark pit and begged, *"Can't there be another way?"*

His sorrow was single and simple—He was to be severed totally from His Father. Jesus was the Word of God. He had never known separation from His Father. The nails weren't the issue. The whips didn't matter. Something greater was at stake.

No gospel account of the passion reflects His physical response to the pains from the crown of thorns, roman whips or even the nails. We aren't told that He cried or screamed. He surely must have, but it wasn't important enough to be recorded. The pain that saved us wasn't physical. It was spiritual anguish.

This was the cup of suffering—total separation from His Father. It is what theologians call 'spiritual death'. Jesus took on our sin nature and became one with Man.

It was at that moment that Jesus introduced us to the most important revelation of God. This was the very essence of His ministry. Now, He could unveil God.

To the modern mind, how He addressed God doesn't make much of an impression, but it is huge to the Jewish mind.

All through His ministry, Jesus caused quite a massive stir in the religious world by referring to God as His Father. He frequently used the Greek word, 'Pater'. This was such a big deal that they wanted to stone Him for blasphemy at some point.

The Jews knew God as Yahweh. It is a name so sacred, holy and exalted that they would not even pronounce the name. It is rendered in the Hebrew Bible with only four consonants: YHWH. When the scribes wanted to write the name, they took a bath, got a new pen, wrote it and then discarded the pen afterwards. They didn't reverence God; they dreaded Him. I don't blame them though. If you saw Uzzah struck dead because he tried to steady the Ark of God, and the Mount Sinai that smoked continuously with fire and thunderings, you would too!

Let me show you this. Most of Jesus' last words on the cross were direct quotes from Psalm 22 and 31.
David addressed Psalm 31 to YHWH (see verse 1, Lord as used there is YHWH) and prophetically said in verse 5:

"Into thine hand I commit my spirit: thou hast redeemed me, O Lord God of truth."

Jesus quotes David but changes whom He addressed.

"And when Jesus had cried with a loud voice, he said, Father, into thy hands I commend my spirit: and having said thus, he gave up the ghost." (Luke 23:46)

David addressed it to the fearsome YHWH, Jesus

addressed it to His loving '*Pater*' (Father).

The transition from YHWH to Father, in seed form, is possibly the aptest summary of the gospel message.

Before the coming of Christ, God was distant and unapproachable. His name could not be spoken nor could you in your wildest imagination think you could have a personal relationship with Him. Now, through the intercession of Christ and His redemptive work, we who were once *"far away have been brought near through the blood of Christ"* (Ephesians 2:13).

Indeed, it is fitting that at the moment Jesus paid the ultimate price with His life and blood, He addressed God as Father, thereby modelling the new way opened to all of us through the gospel—a way into His Family.

Now, we can all cry "Father", for as Paul declares, *"You did not receive a spirit that makes you a slave again to fear, but you received the Spirit of sonship. And by him we cry, 'Abba, Father'"* (Romans 8:15).

This is the good news through the work of Jesus Christ!

BUT WHY ABBA?

For a moment, let's ask, why did He call Him Abba Father? Is there a significance to this? Was Father not enough?

Abba is an Aramaic term with two-fold implications.

First, it was used informally by children for their father, some-thing like "daddy" and "papa". Secondly, it was used by adult children as a term of respect.

The former indicating intimacy, the latter reverence. Slaves were forbidden to address the head of the family by this term.

"Abba" is the word framed by the lips of infants, and signifies complete trust. "Father" expresses an intelligent understanding of the type of relationship.

Both used together expresses the confident love of the child and his rational submission to the Father.

Jesus called Him Abba as a Son, conscious of His position and the love of His Father, yet as a Servant, willingly submitted to His Father's will.

Look at the prayers of Jesus in Gethsemane as recorded in Mark 14:36 again:

"And he said, Abba, Father, all things are possible unto

thee; take away this cup from me: nevertheless not what I will, but what thou wilt."

He was conscious of His sonship, yet submitted as a servant. This is clearer in some recent translations.

"Abba, my Father, *all things are possible for you. Please - don't allow me to drink this cup of suffering!* ***Yet what I want is not important, for I only desire to fulfil your plan for me."***
(TPT)

"Papa, Father, *you can- can't you?- Get me out of this. Take this cup away from me.* ***But please, not what I want- what do you want?"***
(MSG)

Declaring Abba is to call Him Daddy and Lord at the same time. It is the heart cry of sons and the adoration of servants.

This was the ultimate assignment of the incarnate Christ. As the prototype Son, through His sufferings, He has brought many sons into glory.

When we realise the magnitude of His sacrifice and love, we scream, we cry out in wonder and amazement, "Abba Father!"
This realisation compels us to serve. Our service

isn't that of slaves - done out of compulsion. This service is a service of wonder.

The wonder of His love compels us to serve the purposes of His love.

We dare to call Him Abba!
I'm a son who serves.

Embracing the necessity of service without the revelation of sonship produces slaves. Embracing the privileges of sonship without the revelation of servanthood produces "entitled brats".

The highest worship of a son is to serve his Father's purposes.
The highest rebellion of a servant is to seize the rights of sons.

We don't have to choose between our sonship and servanthood. It's not an either/or proposition. God is pleased when our identity is firmly rooted as sons, yet we carry the heart of a servant.

God gifted us sonship.
We gift Him service.

The Christian Faith is a journey between two witnesses from the Father.
First is His private witness, whispering gently in

your heart at the new birth, assuring you that you are His child to which your inner man roars *"Abba, Father!"*

It ends with the public witness of the Father before all of Heaven when He says *"Well done, good and faithful servant."*

Come with me in this book as you discover who you truly are. One thing I can assure you is this—the revelation in the pages of this book will radically alter the course of your life!

Come along...

SECTION ONE

Sonship

"The Lord thy God in the midst of thee is mighty; he will save,

he will rejoice over thee with joy;

he will rest in his love,

he will joy over thee with singing."

ZEPHANIAH 3:17

"My heart beats for you, and my love for you stirs up my pity.

I won't punish you in my anger, and I won't destroy Israel again.

I am God and not a human;

I am the Holy One, and I am among you.

I will not come against you in anger."

HOSEA 11: 8B-9
NCV

The Father Heart Of God

The precision and beauty of creation beggars all description. The mind behind the conceptualisation and workings of this universe has to be the most brilliant mind—the sheer vastness, the stellar rotation, the beautiful planets...

If truly the world as we know it happened by chance, then chance must be the most deliberate reasoning force in the entire universe.

Clearly, nothing was left to chance. This universe isn't the product of chance or happenstance. Creation bears the stroke of a master sculptor.

The first two chapters of the Bible contain some of the most profound phenomena that can ever be studied by scientists. The patient and stepwise approach to the designing of this world is worthy of study and admiration. For example, the lights for photosynthesis were hung in space before the trees were created. Talk of beauty, structure and design!

The earth is one of the smallest of God's creations, yet everything was designed with her in mind. The sun, the moon..., everything functions to maintain life on earth.

God busied Himself through untold ages, preparing a home for His grandest creation.

The focus wasn't the planet earth; she's just a home for God's passion—Man!

Man was the ultimate reason for all creation. If this is true, what then is the reason for man?

The answer is very straightforward: To satisfy the aching, longing, lonely heart of the Great Father, God.

God's passion is not the created universe; you and I are His greatest obsession.

Christianity is just another religion if it doesn't capture the heart of the Father. Religions have gods. Christians have a Father.

Little wonder Paul said, *"For this cause I bow my knees unto the Father of our Lord Jesus Christ, of whom the whole family in heaven and earth is named,"* (Ephesians 3:14-15)

We must capture the heart and attitude of our Father to understand our faith. God craved to have a family. He wanted a home. little wonder, He always came visiting Adam and Eve at the cool of the day.

As glorious as heaven is, God still left all of it to spend time with man. Angels were servants. There's a limit to the communion, fellowship and intimacy you can have with servants. God wanted sons!

Even after the fall of man in the garden, God devised a plan to regain His family, a plan that would take over six thousand years to mature. He patiently worked with the patriarchs, the nation of Israel, and the prophets until the appointed time of redemption came.

I love the way Paul described it,

"But when the right time came, the time God decided on, he sent his Son, born of a woman, born as a Jew, to buy freedom for us who were slaves to the law so that he could adopt us as his very own sons.
And because we are his sons, God has sent the Spirit of his Son into our hearts, **so now we can rightly speak of God as our dear Father.**
Now we are no longer slaves but God's own sons. And since we are his sons, everything he has belongs to us, for that is the way God planned."
(Galatians 4:4-7 TIB)

We are not slaves or servants. We are sons. This is the ultimate desire in the Father's heart. He wanted sons.

Paul again described this drama of love in Hebrews 2:11-13. I particularly like the way The living Bible puts it.

"We who have been made holy by Jesus, now have the same Father he has. That is why Jesus is not ashamed to call us his brothers. For he says in the book of Psalms, "I will talk to my brothers about God my Father, and together we will sing his praises."
At another time he said, "I will put my trust in God along with my brothers." And at still another time,
"See, here am I and the children God gave me."

Friends, if this is remotely true, which it is, then it is too beautiful to appreciate with the human mind.

Christianity is not a religion—it is a family, the family of God. This is the most significant difference between Christianity and all the religions in the world.

Christianity is not man looking for God. It is God looking for man.

From the Garden, God was the Lover who always came visiting.

I remember taking a prayer stroll several years ago

as a medical student, and the Lord stopped me in my tracks and asked, *"since you met God, have you met Daddy?"*

At that time, I couldn't see Him as my Daddy. That was where my journey started.

I'm asking you too; **"Since you met God, have you met Daddy?"**

The vital core of Christianity is the Father-Heart of God. He longs to have a family. This isn't about a God and His subjects; it's about a Father and His kids!

THE PRODIGAL FATHER

The screams and shouts of the woman abruptly stopped. It was replaced with another cry. The smile on the midwife's face as she parted the curtains could not be mistaken. She could only be bringing good news. Everyone erupted in joy as the midwife announced the arrival of a bouncing baby boy.

Laughing hysterically with tears streaming down his cheeks, the boy's father rushed to grab him. This was his second son – his replica. His joy knew no bounds.

Several years later, the boys have become men, and

they had joined the family business. Daddy was a very wealthy man, and in the far east, wealth was kept within the family. The business was the children's inheritance.

Everyone was envious of this family. They were family goals.

In the orient, a man's pride were his sons, but all of this was about to change.

One day, the younger son asked to see his father. Daddy had just retired from a hard day's work. "Can it wait?" he asked, lifting his head for a bit from unlacing his sandals. When he saw his son's face, he knew it couldn't wait. Now, he was concerned and all ears.

The son asked,

"Father, give me the portion of goods that falleth to me...."
(Luke 15:12)

This was the worst day of the father's life. To ask for your inheritance while your father was alive is to wish him dead.

With his heart full of pain, the father obliged him. He divided his properties between his two sons.

We always miss that little detail though—that the father divided it between his sons.

I'm sure you know the story now. A few days later,

the son travelled far away from home and wasted his inheritance. In a short while, he had nothing left and was forced to start taking care of swine. There is no better depiction of the sinner in the gospels. Swine is an abomination to the Jews and taking care of them showed the extreme hardship he suffered.

I want us to study the events that follow carefully.

"And when he came to himself, he said, How many hired servants of my father's have bread enough and to spare, and I perish with hunger! I will arise and go to my father, and will say unto him, Father, I have sinned against heaven, and before thee, And am no more worthy to be called thy son: make me as one of thy hired servants." (Luke 15:17-19)

Please note, this young man wasn't repentant. He was simply hungry, and he planned a way to get back to his father. All he wanted was food, just like many people only want a miracle.

He rehearsed his negotiation pitch, and it sounded perfect to him.

And in that pitch is a very powerful fact. Even hired servants had it better in his father's house than him. He preferred to be a servant in his father's house.

I have always wondered if we truly know what it means to be sons in God's house. Angels are servants.

We are sons.

All the young man wanted was to be restored as a servant.

"And he arose, and came to his father. But when he was yet a great way off, his father saw him, and had compassion, and ran, and fell on his neck, and kissed him. And the son said unto him, Father, I have sinned against heaven, and in thy sight, and am no more worthy to be called thy son."
(Luke 15:20-21)

It was the father who ran to hug the boy. How did he see him from a great way off, save that he was always looking out the window hoping that someday his son would return home? The father had long awaited this day.

"But the father said to his servants, Bring forth the best robe, and put it on him; and put a ring on his hand, and shoes on his feet: And bring hither the fatted calf, and kill it; and let us eat, and be merry: For this my son was dead, and is alive again; he was lost, and is found. And they began to be merry."
(Luke 15:22-24)

The father did three significant things.

He gave him his robe, taking off the uniform of a

hired servant that he had on him. He placed on him the best robe depicting that his sins were forgiven. Right Standing (Righteousness) restored!

Secondly, the father put his signet ring of authority on his hand. This meant that he had his father's authority and could dispense of his father's inheritance at will. Payments were made in those days with this ring. It is akin to a signature on a cheque today. Authority restored!

Thirdly, the father gave him shoes to wear. Only sons wore shoes. Servants walked around barefooted. The shoes were a sign of his relationship with his father. Sonship restored!

What did the son do to deserve his father's love? Nothing!

Actually, that's inaccurate. He did something—He received it.

He accepted all his father did for him. He didn't struggle to prove his guilt, regret, or how undeserving he was; he simply received his father's reckless, unconditional, inexplicable love.

Scriptures like these now make sense against this backdrop:

"Herein is love, not that we loved God, but that he

loved us, and sent his Son to be the propitiation for our sins."
(1 John 4:10)

Love is not measured by how much we love Him but by how much He loved us and how much of that love we have received.

"Behold, what manner of love the Father hath bestowed upon us, that we should be called the sons of God: therefore the world knoweth us not, because it knew him not. Beloved, now are we the sons of God, and it doth not yet appear what we shall be: but we know that, when he shall appear, we shall be like him; for we shall see him as he is."
(1 John 3:1-2)

The Apostle, John, calls on everyone to wonder at this new kind of love God has bestowed on us in making us His sons.

"What manner of" is the Greek word, *'potapen'* which means "from what country, race or tribe". This love is foreign to humans. One writer translates it as, "from what far realms".

"Hath bestowed" is translated from *'dedoken'*, the perfect tense form of *'didomi'* which means "to give something to someone". The tense used here indicates that the gift given becomes the permanent possession of the recipient.

God has placed His love upon the saints in the sense that we have become the permanent objects of His love.

The father in the parable was the prodigal one—reckless with his love! The parable was about the father, not the son.

It depicts the Father Heart of God. His love, His care and personal concern for you and me.

Many Christians today have a religious spirit like the elder brother. He had all the details of his brother's escapades. He is the one who told us that the younger brother wasted his living with harlots. He had many reasons why the father shouldn't forgive his brother.

"And he answering said to his father, Lo, these many years do I serve thee, neither transgressed I at any time thy commandment: and yet thou never gavest me a kid, that I might make merry with my friends: But as soon as this thy son was come, which hath devoured thy living with harlots, thou hast killed for him the fatted calf. And he said unto him, Son, thou art ever with me, and all that I have is thine. It was meet that we should make merry, and be glad: for this thy brother was dead, and is alive again; and was lost, and is found."
(Luke 15:29 -32)

Notice that he won't even associate with him as a brother. He said "this thy son". He was full of self-righteousness. As far as he was concerned, except you worked for it, you didn't deserve it. But in the father's economy, no one can ever work to earn it.

It is all grace, and it is received by faith. This is the gospel. Now are we sons of God!

Jesus, The Language Of God

A GOD IN MAN'S IMAGE

Man has always created a 'god' that fits his image. Most times, man views God through his lens and projects his image on Him. This is one of the biggest hindrances to folks believing the gospel wholeheartedly. It's almost impossible to believe the claims of the gospel about God when all our experiences with people point to the opposite.

God created man in His image. Man has returned the favour to God by creating a 'god' in his image.

Now, we see a god that needs to be 'pursued' in ceaseless fastings and prayers before he can be known, a god that needs you to please him before he accepts you, a god that needs you to obey him before he blesses you.

One of the earliest recorded examples of man creating a god in his image is that of the children of Israel journeying through the wilderness.

Moses had taken seventy men with him to the mountain to meet with God on His invitation. He was gone for forty days and forty nights. The truth is, that was a long time to leave the children of Israel.

The wilderness was not a safe place; it was dangerous. Usually, you'd have robbers attacking travellers, killing and hurting everyone in sight while dispossessing them of their goods.

When the Israelites were leaving Egypt, God had instructed them to take as much as they wanted from the Egyptians, who didn't object because they wanted them out of their country.

This nation of slaves left Egypt very wealthy—fully supplied. All the nations around knew what had happened to Egypt, so no nation was friendly with Israel.

In the wilderness, Israel was a sitting target. A wealthy nation without friends or a defined military was easy prey.

It is humanly understandable that the Israelites were afraid and that they needed some form of assurance since the man who had a direct line to God had been gone for more than a month with no idea of his return date.

Here's Moses' account:

"And when the people saw that Moses delayed to come down out of the mount, the people gathered themselves together unto Aaron, and said unto him, Up, make us gods, which shall go before us; for as for this Moses, the man that brought us up out of the land of Egypt, we wot not what is become of him.

And Aaron said unto them, Break off the golden earrings, which are in the ears of your wives, of your sons, and of your daughters, and bring them unto me. And all the people brake off the golden earrings which were in their ears, and brought them unto Aaron. And he received them at their hand, and fashioned it with a graving tool, after he had made it a molten calf: and they said, These be thy gods, O Israel, which brought thee up out of the land of Egypt.

And when Aaron saw it, he built an altar before it; and Aaron made proclamation, and said, Tomorrow is a feast to the Lord. And they rose up early on the morrow, and offered burnt offerings, and brought peace offerings; and the people sat down to eat and to drink, and rose up to

play."
(Exodus 32:1-6)

Here is what's intriguing. How did Israel know what God looked like? I mean, yes, they wanted a symbol, something they could see to believe that they had some divine presence with them, but what are the odds that a calf would have been the chosen symbolism for God?

Why not a statue of Moses?

They simply reproduced an image they had seen in Egypt. Egypt had several gods depicted as animals.

Israel was far removed from Egypt, but their concept of God was the image they were used to—an image from Egypt.

Many Believers are like this. It's a difficult task for them to see God for who He truly is.

We define God by our societal construct, experiences or even what we were told in Sunday school.

The question is who God is. Is He knowable? Is He a mysterious being out there in space that we just hope hears us when we pray?

As a kid, I read from an author I respected that God plays hide and seek with us. He never lets us know Him truly. I was young and not so learned in scriptures, but

I knew better than to believe that.

WHO OR WHAT IS GOD?

The Old Testament is filled with several accounts of the mighty acts of God and several stories of God meeting the pressing needs of His people. If you asked two different individuals, they would have completely different revelations of God.

For example, in Genesis 1:1, Moses introduces God as the Elohim. Elohim is the name of God associated with creation.

Further down in Genesis 14, God reveals Himself to Abraham as the El Elyon, the Most High God. Abraham had gone to war against four nations and their armies, taking three hundred and eighteen servants trained in his house who weren't men of war, but he was victorious. God showed Himself to be higher than any human king.

Later on, God introduces Himself afresh to Abraham as the El Shaddai in Genesis 17:1.

"And when Abram was ninety years old and nine, the Lord appeared to Abram, and said unto him, I am the Almighty God; walk before me, and be thou perfect."

El Shaddai, the Almighty God, is literally translated

the strong and many breasted one. He was the God that brought nourishment, fruitfulness and multiplication to Abraham. He was physically infertile, so God showed up in his life as what he needed – the Provider. Much more than just giving him an offspring, it was God's goal to raise a nation through Abraham. Multiplication was the need, so El Shaddai showed up.

We can go on and on, but I want you to see something interesting here in Exodus 6:

"Then the Lord said unto Moses, Now shalt thou see what I will do to Pharaoh: for with a strong hand shall he let them go, and with a strong hand shall he drive them out of his land. And God spake unto Moses, and said unto him, I am the Lord: And I appeared unto Abraham, unto Isaac, and unto Jacob, by the name of God Almighty, but by my name Jehovah was I not known to them."
(Exodus 6:1-3)

God reveals Himself as Jehovah YHWH, to Moses. This is the redemptive name of God. It denotes a God who binds Himself by covenant to His people. Over time, God builds on this revelation, indicating the redemptive blessings He brings into our lives.

But that's not my focus here. Observe that God says He revealed Himself to Abraham, Isaac and Jacob as El Shaddai but not as Jehovah.

So, if you asked them who Jehovah was, they would

be absolutely clueless! Only Moses had that revelation. Yet it was the same God they all met.

The God of Abraham was radically different from the God of Moses.

Man was spiritually dead and could not have a relationship with God. He had no means of receiving the knowledge of God.

Thus, God had to reveal Himself to man based on his needs. He became what man needed, and that formed the basis for their conceptual knowledge of God.

Here's the problem. God is not Jehovah Rophe, the Healer. That's what He does. He heals.

He is not Jehovah Jireh, the Provider. That's what He does. He provides.

This is sense knowledge—knowledge gathered by what you have felt and experienced, but the true knowledge of God comes by revelation to the human spirit.

These Old Testament concepts are WHAT God does, not WHO He is.

I desire that Believers understand this—that these revelations of God in the Old Testament aren't revelations in the truest sense. They are not the names of God. They are descriptions of what He does.

There's a vast difference between nature and

function. The question is, what is His nature? Who is God?

Jesus made a statement that helps solve this riddle:

"And no man hath ascended up to heaven, but he that came down from heaven, even the Son of man which is in heaven."
(John 3:13)

No man has seen the Father save He that came down from heaven. He's the only one qualified to reveal Him to us.

Apostle Paul agrees to this. This is how he put it:

"God, who at sundry times and in divers manners spake in time past unto the fathers by the prophets,
Hath in these last days spoken unto us by his Son, whom he hath appointed heir of all things, by whom also he made the worlds;"
(Hebrews 1:1)

The New Testament was mostly written in Greek, so I usually reference it in my studies. It helps with the proper and better interpretation of the text.

Reading this verse in Greek, the literal rendering is,

"At sundry times and in divers manners God spake to the fathers by means of the prophets."

The Greeks place important words at the beginning of a sentence for emphasis. In this text, the emphasis is not that God spoke but the way and manner in which He spoke.

'*Sundry times*' is translated from the Greek word '*polumeros*', meaning "many parts or many portions".
The revelations were also given "*in diverse manners*" which is translated from the Greek word '*polutropos*' meaning "different manners, many ways or varying modes".

God communicated to the fathers through the prophets in many portions—the revelation of God was progressive. He revealed bits and bits of Himself over time. No man had access to the fullness.
Secondly, He spoke in different modes - some were in poetry, others in prose, or laws, etc.

Paul contrasts the revelation of God in the Old Testament with the New Testament. Let's read on:

"*Hath in these last days spoken unto us by [his] Son, whom he hath appointed heir of all things, by whom also he made the worlds;*"
(Hebrews 1:2)

Understanding what Paul was saying in these two verses changes everything. It is the difference between

Christianity and Judaism. Many Believers are adherents of the ideals of Judaism.

First, God has spoken. He is not speaking. The canon of truth and revelation is closed. There is a finality on truth now.

Every single revelation we have must align with what '**God has spoken**'.

You will never need a prophet to hear God! God has spoken!

Remember the emphasis in verse one—it isn't that God spoke but the manner in which He spoke. So, in what manner did He speak in these last days?

In Son.

Please note that the word 'his' before Son in verse two is italicised which means it wasn't in the original manuscript but was added by the translators because they assumed it would give the verse more grammatical sense. But it was unnecessary. As we study further, you'd understand.

'God spake in Son'. I know this is not proper English but here's what Paul was saying,

1. The Son is the message
2. Sonship is the nature (content) of the message

This becomes clearer when you study some newer translations of the Bible:

"In many separate revelations [each of which set forth a portion of the Truth] and in different ways God spoke of old to [our] forefathers in and by the prophets,
[But] in the last of these days ***He has spoken to us in [the person of a] Son,*** *Whom He appointed Heir and lawful Owner of all things, also by and through Whom He created the worlds and the reaches of space and the ages of time [He made, produced, built, operated, and arranged them in order]."*
(Hebrews 1:1-2 AMPC)

"God, having spoken to the fathers long ago in [the voices and writings of] the prophets in many separate revelations [each of which set forth a portion of the truth], and in many ways, has in these last days ***spoken [with finality] to us in [the person of One who is by His character and nature] His Son [namely Jesus],*** *whom He appointed heir and lawful owner of all things, through whom also He created the universe [that is, the universe as a space-time-matter continuum]."*
(Hebrews 1:1-2 AMP)

"Throughout our history God has spoken to our ancestors by his prophets in many different ways. The revelation he gave them was only a fragment at a time, building one truth upon another.

But to us living in these last days, **God now speaks to us openly in the language of a Son,** *the appointed Heir of everything, for through him God created the panorama of all things and all time."*
(Hebrews 1:1-2 TPT)

1. The Son Is The Message

Jesus didn't bring us a message from Heaven. God didn't send Him to tell us something. He, Jesus, was the message. He came to reveal the Father to us. Remember He said to Philip, *"he that hath seen me hath seen the Father; and how sayest thou then, Shew us the Father?"*

No prophet claimed to be a revelation of God. Only Jesus! They all claimed to have a message from God. His claims were higher. Little wonder they crucified Him for blasphemy. How could a man claim to be one with God? (John 10:30)

Jesus never said, *"thus saith the lord"*. He was the Lord!

Someone best said it: "Jesus, the Language of God!"

All revelation ends in Jesus. All revelation is Jesus.
God gave Moses a vision. Jesus was the vision.
God gave Isaiah a message. Jesus was the message.
God gave David a song. Jesus was the song.

All questions about God end with finality in Jesus.

Jesus was God in the flesh.

"In the beginning was the Word, and the Word was with God, and the Word was God. The same was in the beginning with God. All things were made by him; and without him was not anything made that was made.
And the Word was made flesh, and dwelt among us, (and we beheld his glory, the glory as of the only begotten of the Father,) full of grace and truth."
(John 1:1-3, 14)

John uses a curious term here—'*Logos*'. This word didn't exist in the Jewish vocabulary. He borrowed it from the learned Greeks. Their philosophers were the first to use it. They used it to describe the intelligence that they believed must have created the world. They didn't believe in God but believed there was an intelligence controlling the world.

This '*logos*', John says, is God. '*Logos*' is the sum total of all His thoughts, imaginations, ideas and words. This '*logos*' became flesh—Jesus.

Jesus was the Word of God made flesh. In essence, He is the sum total of all God's thoughts, imaginations, ideas and words. All!

Jesus was the will of God made flesh. God has no will outside Jesus. He came to reveal the heart of the Father to us.

To see Jesus is to know God.

He loved sinners. He healed the sick. He provided for material needs. He raised the dead. These and more are the Will of God!

God does not teach with sickness. He spoke once and for all in Jesus—there's no new lesson to be learnt.

2. Sonship is the nature and character of the Message

God has never been about religion; He's always been about family. God sent Jesus as a Son—not a fiery prophet nor a powerful angel.

Sonship is the message. It is the nature and character of the message. Christianity isn't a religion. Far from it! Very far. You cannot understand these truths and think of it as a religion. Impossible!

Jesus came to show us the possibility of man becoming the offspring of God. You don't have to die to attain special sainthood. Now, are we the sons of God.

This is the message- the Father Heart of God seeking out sons.

"For it became him, for whom are all things, and by whom

are all things, in bringing many sons unto glory, to make the captain of their salvation perfect through sufferings."
(Hebrews 2:10)

"Behold, what manner of love the Father hath bestowed upon us, that we should be called the sons of God: therefore the world knoweth us not, because it knew him not. Beloved, now are we the sons of God, and it doth not yet appear what we shall be: but we know that, when he shall appear, we shall be like him; for we shall see him as he is."
(1 John 3:1-2)

This is the message—He came that we may be made sons of God in the same way He is a Son of God.

This is the Gospel—that God in search of sons sacrificed His only begotten Son. Israel was a nation of servants. Zion is a nation of sons.

Slaves own nothing. Sons own everything.

I love what Jesus said as He ascended to heaven,

"...but go to my brethren, and say unto them, I ascend unto my Father, and your Father; and to my God, and your God."
(John 20:17)

Now, He's not my Father alone; He's now your

Father too! Notice that He declared Him to be Father before calling Him God.

Never ever change this order again.

To the Believer, He's first a Father who loves us dearly before He's a God we serve. To the world, He's a God to be feared and served, and never to be disrespected by being referred to as a Father.

Jesus, The Pattern Son

A HOUSE OF SONS

*"Wherefore, holy brethren, partakers of the heavenly calling, consider the Apostle and High Priest of our profession, Christ Jesus; Who was faithful to him that appointed him, as also Moses was faithful in all his house. For this man was counted worthy of more glory than Moses, inasmuch as he who hath builded the house hath more honour than the house. For every house is builded by some man; but he that built all things is God. **And Moses verily was faithful in all his house, as a servant**, for a testimony of those things which were to be spoken after; **But Christ as a son over his own house; whose house are we,...**"*
(Hebrews 3:1-6)

The writer of the book of Hebrews is a brilliant communicator. Hebrews is a book of comparisons to prove one point—Jesus and the New Covenant cut in His blood are greater than anything that ever preexisted.

In this chapter, the writer takes on the delicate task of comparing Moses and Jesus, the Messiah.

To you, that might not mean much, but his audience was Jewish, and they had the deepest regard for Moses. They could stone you to death for undermining Moses. Although his readers were now Christians, he still had to be cautious.

Tactfully, the writer first states that both the Messiah and Moses were faithful to God. This drops their guards, making it easy for him to pass the real message—that the Messiah is greater than Moses.

He asserts that Moses was faithful as a servant, but Jesus was faithful as the Son. Moses was a servant in the house of God. Jesus was a Son over the house.

Moses and Jesus represented two dispensations. Thus, it follows that since Jesus is better than Moses, the testament that He initiated must be better than the one Moses was instrumental in bringing.

I love the development of the thoughts in verses 5 and 6 as it appears in the Amplified Classic Bible:

"And Moses certainly was faithful in the administration of all God's house [but it was only] as a ministering servant. [In his entire ministry he was but] a testimony to the things which were to be spoken [the revelations to be given afterward in Christ].
But Christ (the Messiah) was faithful over His [own Father's] house as a Son [and Master of it]. And it is we who are [now members] of this house,..."
(Hebrews 3:5-6 AMPC)

The first testament was handed to a servant, the second and last testament to a Son.

More importantly, is the choice of the Greek word for 'house' that Paul uses here, '*oikos*'. While it directly means a dwelling place, it also refers to a lineage or a race of people like when you say 'the house of Israel.' The house of Israel implies that there's a people or nation called Israel or a people who are descendants of a man named Israel (Jacob).

The house of Moses refers to a people who descended from Moses, and the house of Jesus refers to a people who descended from Jesus.

Moses was a servant, so by extension, his house was a house of servants.
Jesus is the Son—His house is a house of sons.
The implications of this are far-reaching!

The Old Testament is an account of the exploits of servants. Israel was a nation of servants. The prophets were servants. The patriarchs were servants. At best, God called them friends.

Moses, a servant, parted the red sea with his rod.
Joshua, a servant, commanded the sun to stand still, and it obeyed.
Daniel, a servant, was thrown into the lion's den and came out unhurt.
They were all servants!

But we are of the house of Jesus - a house of sons. We are not slaves nor servants; we are born sons. We are born free.

Jesus declared that John the Baptist was the greatest prophet who ever lived. He was greater than Isaiah, Jeremiah, Moses, and all other prophets before him. The reason is simple. He had the honour of being the forerunner of the Messiah and the honour of baptising Him. All the other prophets prophesied the coming of the Messiah, only John saw Him.

He was the last leg in the prophetic relay, and you know that you run your best leg last.

Yet Jesus said unapologetically, the least in this new kingdom, this house of sons, is greater than John!

"Verily I say unto you, Among them that are born of

women there hath not risen a greater than John the Baptist: **notwithstanding he that is least in the kingdom of heaven is greater than he.***"*
(Matthew 11:11)

I like to put it this way,

The greatest servant is still a servant.
The least son is still a son.
A servant in all of his glories is nothing comparable to a son in all of his mess.

A great servant is, at best, the greatest servant. At no time will a servant be better than a son.

Little wonder He called us brethren because this is a house of sons.

"For it became him, for whom are all things, and by whom are all things, **in bringing many sons unto glory***, to make the captain of their salvation perfect through sufferings.* **For both he that sanctifieth and they who are sanctified are all of one: for which cause he is not ashamed to call them brethren***, Saying, I will declare thy name unto my brethren, in the midst of the Church will I sing praise unto thee.*
And again, I will put my trust in him. And again, **Behold I and the children which God hath given me.***"*
(Hebrews 2:10-13)

He that sanctifies and the sanctified are one—of the same stock, cut from the same cloth.

If the sanctifying Messiah is a Son, then we the sanctified are sons, and He is proud to associate with us.

The men in the Old Testament achieved outstanding feats that still marvels us. They were servants.

How much more sons?

The exploits of the servants were recorded so that the sons may raise their sights and choose the higher life in Christ.

One of Isaiah's most quoted prophecies is about servants, not sons!

"No weapon that is formed against thee shall prosper; and every tongue that shall rise against thee in judgment thou shalt condemn.
This is the heritage of the servants of the Lord , *and their righteousness is of me, saith the Lord. "*
(Isaiah 54:17)

If this is meant for servants, what then is the heritage of sons?

I believe that in these last days, God is flooding our hearts with the revelation of who we are and what

Christ has made us in God. The knowledge of who we are will eliminate many prayer points and end the faith struggles of many Believers.

Now are we sons of God in the order of Jesus. Not tomorrow. Not when we get to heaven. Now!

Christ gave us the status of sonship with all its attendant privileges. Now! Not in the sweet by-and-by.

*"Behold, what manner of love the Father hath bestowed upon us, that we should be called the sons of God: therefore the world knoweth us not, because it knew him not. Beloved, **now are we the sons of God**, and it doth not yet appear what we shall be: but we know that, when he shall appear, we shall be like him; for we shall see him as he is."*
(1 John 3:1-2)

I want the scriptures to speak to you for itself. I won't run commentaries on these verses, but I will present them to you in several translations.

"See what [an incredible] quality of love the Father has given (shown, bestowed on) us, that we should [be permitted to] be named and called and counted the children of God! And so we are! The reason that the world does not know (recognize, acknowledge) us is that it does not know (recognize, acknowledge) Him.

*Beloved, **we are [even here and] now God's children**; it is not yet disclosed (made clear) what we shall be [hereafter], but we know that when He comes and is manifested, we shall [as God's children] resemble and be like Him, for we shall see Him just as He [really] is."*
(AMPC)

*"See how very much our heavenly Father loves us, for he allows us to be called his children—think of it—and we really are! But since most people don't know God, naturally they don't understand that we are his children. **Yes, dear friends, we are already God's children, right now**, and we can't even imagine what it is going to be like later on. But we do know this, that when he comes we will be like him, as a result of seeing him as he really is."*
(TLB)

You see, sonship was the plan right from the beginning. Adam was the son of God. God always wanted a family, so He created a son for fellowship.

"Which was the son of Enos, which was the son of Seth, which was the son of Adam, which was the son of God."
(Luke 3:38)

God never wanted it any other way, but sin came in and corrupted the plan. Sons became servants, but by the sacrifice of Jesus on the cross, He made a way unto the Father and into His family.

JESUS, THE ONLY AND THE FIRST

When you study through the Gospels and the Epistles, you notice that Jesus was referred to as both the only begotten and as the first begotten Son. There's no contradiction here at all.

Actually, seeming contradictions in scriptures are the backdrop against which personal revelation is birthed.

Grammatically it is incorrect to refer to something as the first and yet only at the same time. To be first presupposes that there's a next. However, we know that with Jesus, He can be A and Z at the same time. The same who is the lion is the lamb. He is only yet first.

The Sacrifice-Son—The Only Begotten.

"For God so loved the world, that he gave his only begotten Son, that whosoever believeth in him should not perish, but have everlasting life."
(John 3:16)

Begotten as used here and in several other instances is from the Greek word *'monogenes'*.

'Monogenes' is drawn from these two roots; *'mono'*, meaning "the original, the sole, the only one (Son)" and *'ginomai'*, meaning "to cause to be, to generate."

Casually, it would mean the only child indicating that there's none other. Because of this, several preachers have taught that Jesus was the only begotten, and then later, He became the first begotten when we Believers were born again in Him.

That seems right and true until you study the use of that word in other contexts.

For example, '*monogenes*' was used for Isaac. If it were about being the only child as we have said of Jesus, this wouldn't be true with Isaac. He was never an only child. Ishmael should have been the one to be referred to as a '*monogenes*'.

"By faith Abraham, when he was tried, offered up Isaac: and he that had received the promises offered up his only begotten (monogenes) son."
(Hebrew 11:17)

This is quite similar to what God said when He asked Abraham to offer up Isaac.

*"And he said, Take now thy son, **thine only son Isaac**, whom thou lovest, and get thee into the land of Moriah; and offer him there for a burnt offering upon one of the mountains which I will tell thee of."*
(Genesis 22:2)

If your knowledge of Old Testament history is

intact, you know that Ishmael was born before Isaac. Therefore, if '*monogenes*' has no further implication than merely being the only born of a family, then Isaac was never, at any point, the '*monogenes*' of Abraham.

The reference to Isaac as only begotten of Abraham must be in connection with a higher purpose.

Remember that Isaac foreshadowed Jesus as a sacrifice offered on the very same mountain range where Jesus was crucified.

The whole episode on Mount Moriah was figurative of the sacrifice of Jesus.

What we see in 'type' of Isaac is first and foremost applicable to the person and work of Jesus.

Jesus, being the only-begotten Son of God, is much more than being an only child.

It is an unveiling of His unique, inimitable and distinctive character as the Sacrifice-Son.

Jesus was, and is, and ever shall be THE ONLY — BEGOTTEN SON OF GOD as He is the one and only son that was the perfect and final sacrifice for sins.

We are sons, but we are not the only-begotten sons.

The Pattern Son—The First Begotten.

"*And from Jesus Christ, who is the faithful witness, and* **the first begotten of the dead,** *and the prince of the kings*

of the earth. Unto him that loved us, and washed us from our sins in his own blood,"
(Revelation 1:5)

The Apostle, John, had a visitation from the Lord, and here Jesus re-introduces Himself to a man that could claim to have known him very well. This was the one who called himself "the disciple that Jesus loved."

He had a special bond with the Lord while He walked the face of the earth.

Jesus describes Himself to him as the first begotten from the dead—the first man to be born out of spiritual death.

Paul in his epistle to the Colossians says the same,

"And he is the head of the body, the Church: who is the beginning, the firstborn from the dead; that in all thing he might have the pre-eminence."
(Colossians 1:18)

Because of Adam's transgression, all men were spiritually dead—a state of total separation from God and identification with satan's nature.

God's justice couldn't overlook sin, yet God's mercy couldn't overlook you. So, in the most spectacular move of all ages, God judged your sins in Christ, thus upholding His Justice and Mercy.

Jesus, the man full of grace and truth was the only suitable sacrifice for the redemption of man.

By His death, we were justified, declared not guilty.

By His resurrection, we were born anew, out of sin and death, into the life and love of the Father.

"For whom he did foreknow, he also did predestinate to be conformed to the image of his Son, that he might be the firstborn among many brethren."
(Romans 8:29)

The term 'firstborn' is very important to the Believer. Jesus is the firstborn among many brethren.

Paul uses the Greek word, *'prototokos'*. While the definition of the word includes being first in the order of birth, it means much more than that. Jesus is included in this basic definition as He was the first to be born out of spiritual death. Much more, *'prototokos'* means the first sample of a product or better still, a prototype.

'Prototokos' is the name of the Resurrected Christ.

"But God raised him from the dead: And he was seen many days of them which came up with him from Galilee to Jerusalem, who are his witnesses unto the people. And we declare unto you glad tidings, how that the promise which was made unto the fathers, God hath fulfilled the

same unto us their children, in that he hath raised up Jesus again; as it is also written in the second psalm, Thou art my Son, this day have I begotten thee."
(Acts 13:30–33)

God begot Christ again at His resurrection. This is the born again experience. He was the first man to be born again, the first of this new race of recreated beings.

The Resurrected Jesus is the prototype of these new creations of God.

"And declared to be the Son of God with power, according to the spirit of holiness, by the resurrection from the dead:"
(Romans 1:4)

Not only was Christ resurrected from the dead, but through His resurrection, we were regenerated!

"Blessed be the God and Father of our Lord Jesus Christ, which according to his abundant mercy hath begotten us again unto a lively hope by the resurrection of Jesus Christ from the dead,"
(1 Peter 1:3)

Paul declared that the Believer is conformed to the image of the Son (Romans 8:29). It means to fashion alike, to jointly form.

When the Son was formed, we were formed. We were fashioned exactly like Jesus.

Put simply, in Christ's resurrection, He was not only born to be God's firstborn Son, but we also became His brethren.

Please note, that the Jesus who walked the streets of Galilee isn't the prototype— the Resurrected Christ is the prototype. We are recreated after the order of the Risen Jesus and are beneficiaries of His sonship status.

We are the people David prophesied about saying,

"This shall be written for the generation to come: and **the people which shall be created** *shall praise the Lord."* (Psalm 102:918)

The Spirit Of Adoption

Every country has its spiritual heroes and legends. Benson Idahosa was one of the Nigerian heroes. This great man has impacted practically all ministries in Nigeria.

The documented miracles and stories of the audacity of his faith made me wonder if he truly was human. My curiosity led me to read all I could find about him.

One time, I heard him say something like this, "when God was alone in Benin it was a forest, but when I joined God, look at how it has become a city full of Churches."

My young mind struggled with his audacity. I felt he was proud, and his sayings seemed borderline blasphemous.

Then I read that the Prophet of God, T.L. Osborn, once said, "God needs me as much as I need Him".

T. L. Osborn was one of Archbishop Idahosa's mentors.

While I struggled with their audacity, I couldn't deny the hand of God upon their lives.

No evangelist in history had the results I had read and seen in the ministry of T.L. and Daisy Osborn. Same could be said of the Archbishop.

One story about the Archbishop stood out for me—his encounter with witches.

Several years ago, all the witches in the world met in Chicago, and at that meeting, they decided to hold their first world conference in Africa. They chose the city of Benin in Nigeria!

Benin City was known to be the foothold of witches and occult activities in Nigeria before the penetration of the gospel.

Their chief host held a press conference informing journalists and broadcast stations that the first universal conference of witches and wizards would hold in Benin City.

The news got to Benson Idahosa to which he retorted, "What? A world conference of witches? Where?" Benin City was home to Benson Idahosa, and his ministry was situated there.

"It cannot be true because it is NOT possible."

The press asked him what was not possible.

He answered them that the witches from all over the world could not come to Benin City.

Then they asked what he would do to them if they came.

He replied, "I would kill them all."

The press reached out to the chief host.

"Dr Benson Idahosa says your world conference of witches cannot hold in Benin-City." The Chief host responded cynically, "Not even God can stop it." He boasted that he was a wizard, and he knew the efficacy of their power.

This statement headlined many national dailies.

Idahosa's reply never ceases to amaze me. He said, "He is correct. God does not need to waste His time stopping witches from coming to Benin City for a conference. That is why I am here. The Lord does not need to consider matters as trivial as the stopping of a conference of witches."

Well, the rest they say is history. The meeting was cancelled because of one man. All the witches in the world couldn't withstand one man.

The audacity to say that God did not need to get involved always bugs my mind. He had a consciousness that's alien to many Christians today.

Many Believers wish and pray God will help them; this man said God shouldn't bother. He, Idahosa, can take care of business!

I am fully persuaded that He had a revelation of sonship—The Spirit of Adoption. This is what Paul taught in the Bible. It's the crux of the Pauline revelation. This is the goal of redemption.

Ministry gifts are given to teach Believers who they are in Christ, what they have become in Him, and what they can do.

This is what Paul described as coming *"unto a perfect man, unto the measure of the stature of the fulness of Christ:"* (Ephesians 4:13b)

There was a practice in the Roman culture that summed up this idea, *'huiothesia'*. It means, "the placing as an adult son". It is translated in the scriptures as the adoption of sons.

Paul was the only New Testament writer that used this term.

*"For ye have not received the spirit of bondage again to fear; but ye have received **the Spirit of adoption**, whereby we cry, Abba, Father. The Spirit itself beareth witness with our spirit, that we are the children of God: And if children, then heirs; heirs of God, and joint-heirs with Christ;..."*
(Romans 8:15-17a)

*"Having predestinated us unto **the adoption of children** by Jesus Christ to himself, according to the good pleasure of his will, To the praise of the glory of his grace, wherein he hath made us accepted in the beloved."*
(Ephesians 1:5)

It is key to establish from the outset that the Roman practice of adoption isn't in any way similar to what obtains in our modern world. Many wrong teachings have stemmed from overlooking the cultural context in which Paul wrote his epistle.

God didn't go to an orphanage to adopt us and then placed us in His family after signing the papers. No!

In our day and time, an adopted child doesn't bear the nature and genetic makeup of his new parents. He is connected legally to his adopters, but he remains connected by nature to his biological parents.

This doesn't capture the essence of our Redemption. Through the sacrifice of Jesus on the cross, the nature of sin was completely destroyed, and now we are bearers of God's divine nature.

Adoption in the Roman Empire was a complex process, and it varied between different cultures and levels of society.

We'll see some clues that will help us understand the concept of adoption when we study the New Testament history, and the historical cum geographical context within which Paul wrote his epistles.

First, The Gentile Churches of Ephesus, Rome and Galatia each had substantial legal and cultural connections to Rome. Rome was, of course, the capital of the empire. Two of the major cities in Galatia were Roman colonies. Ephesus was the capital of the Roman province, with a Roman governor and about 3,000 Roman soldiers. So Paul was clearly writing about the Roman adoption of sons.

Secondly, the first five emperors of the Roman Empire—the Julio-Claudian dynasty—became emperors by the adoption of sons' process: Augustus, Tiberius, Caligula, Claudius, and Nero.

This provided a realtime illustration for Paul's reading audience in Rome, Galatia and Ephesus.

Adoption of sons was done to provide an heir to the throne of the empire, a seat in the senate or the heir of a family business. The Roman senate approved the adoption of the new heir to the throne, and the approval was conducted publicly in front of seven official witnesses.

It was only after the son had gone through a rigorous training process aimed at conforming the thoughts of the son to the new father such that the son will think exactly like his new father. After that process, it is said that the son has the spirit (mind) of

THE SPIRIT OF ADOPTION

the father.

Adoption of sons in the Roman Empire resulted in some things.

First, the ties of the adopted son to his old family was severed. He lost all the rights in his old family and gained more rights than a natural-born son. The security and protection of an adopted son were vastly superior to that of a natural-born son!

Sometimes, a natural-born son was adopted. Solomon was David's adopted son. Even though he wasn't the first born son and he was the product of an illegitimate union, yet he was the choice.

That's what Solomon meant when he said, *"For I was my father's son, tender and only beloved in the sight of my mother."* (Proverbs 4:3)

Solomon wasn't the only son, but he was the adopted son.

The adopted son became an heir to his new father's estate, even if other sons were born afterwards.

The history and account of the old life of the adopted son were completely wiped out so that the adopted son now becomes a new person entering into a new life. Any prior family connections, past criminal history and/or debts were eliminated.

Even if the adopted son wasn't biologically born,

through this ceremony, he literally and absolutely becomes the son of his new father.

But God tweaked it for us. First, He birthed us through the resurrection of Jesus, justifying us from all sins and guilt, and declared us His sons by birth and by nature. Immediately He placed us as sons, He legally adopting us into His estate.

This makes more sense when you read how Paul contrasted the dispensation of the law and the new dispensation of grace in Galatians 4.

"Now I say, as long as the heir is a child, he does not differ at all from a slave although he is owner of everything, but he is under guardians and managers until the date set by the father.
So also we, while we were children, were held in bondage under the elemental things of the world. But when the fullness of the time came, God sent forth His Son, born of a woman, born under the Law, ***so that He might redeem those who were under the Law, that we (the Gentiles) might receive the adoption as sons.***
Because you are sons, God has sent forth the Spirit of His Son into our hearts, crying, "Abba! Father!"
Therefore you are no longer a slave, but a son; and if a son, then an heir through God."
(Galatians 4:1-7)

Israel was the heir that was a child, placed under the law. God fast-tracked everything for us Gentiles and brings us in at the point of the adoption.

Notice how Paul beautifully presents the case for the Jew and the Gentile. He said God sent forth His son to redeem those under the law, that is Israel, and at the very same time, we the Gentiles received the adoption of sons.

Naturally, that doesn't happen at the same time. The child needs to be at least 18 years of age before he is eligible for the adoption ceremony. But not in this kingdom. The day we are redeemed is the day we are adopted.

That explains why the least in God's kingdom is greater than John the Baptist. They were slaves; we are adopted sons.

Instead of being children under the law who needed a code to guide their conduct, we became adult sons who have the Spirit of the Father leading us.

Now, we have the mind of Christ and the Spirit of the Father dwelling within us and leading us. We are not slaves; we are sons with the rights of sonship.

Adoption is the process whereby God takes the redeemed and justified in Christ and places them as mature sons, instantly bestowing them with full

legal rights of sonship and an unreserved entitlement to all the estate and inheritance of the Father.

We don't grow into this sonship. We are born into it.
We only grow in our understanding of our newfound position in Christ—sonship.

All Believers are adopted sons—mature sons. The difference is in our revelation.

After the completion of the adoption ceremony, the father was rarely seen in the public. His son represented him after that.

The father and the son became one.

The adopted son took over the stewardship and management of his father's estate. In essence, he retired his father and would only involve him in matters that are within his exclusive jurisdiction.

He was trusted with decision-making. His choices were deemed to be as good as his father's. He had a sense of responsibility but not servile dependence.

You then understand why Benson Idahosa and T.L. Osborn made some of those statements. They were conscious of their status as adopted sons.

This is the Gospel—now are we sons. Stop

functioning with a spirit of slavery and bondage that leads to fear. We reverence God, but we do not fear Him like a rattlesnake. No!

You are a son, totally forgiven, guiltless before Him, and He trusts you so much to commit His entire estate into your hands.

Many people think they have to merit it and prove themselves to God before He can relate with them like this. First things first, no man will ever meet God's standards. So God met His own standards in Jesus and credited that to your account. This was what Abraham our Father discovered.

"What shall we say then that Abraham our father, as pertaining to the flesh, hath found? For if Abraham were justified by works, he hath whereof to glory; but not before God. For what saith the scripture?
Abraham believed God, and it was counted unto him for righteousness. *Now to him that worketh is the reward not reckoned of grace, but of debt.*
But to him that worketh not, but believeth on him that justifieth the ungodly, his faith is counted for righteousness.
Even as David also describeth the blessedness of the man, unto whom God imputeth righteousness without works, Saying, Blessed are they whose iniquities are forgiven, and whose sins are covered.

Blessed is the man to whom the Lord will not impute sin. "
(Romans 4:1-8)

Observe this, Abraham believed God, and it was counted unto him for righteousness. He didn't merit it. He didn't work hard at it. He only believed God!

That's all.
Believe and receive that which God has done for you!

Your realisation of who you are will change what you do. Many people are trying to change their conduct without changing their identity.

If I could prove to you that you are remotely related to the Queen of England, your demeanour, conduct and gait will change. There are certain habits you'd immediately stop without effort. Why? Now you know who you are.

Identity is a big issue. We live or fall to who we think we are.

Jesus handed over his entire estate and all that He came to do to a bunch of hard-hearted fellows. Let me show you.

*"Afterward he appeared unto the eleven as they sat at meat, **and upbraided them with their unbelief and***

hardness of heart, because they believed not them which had seen him after he was risen.

And he said unto them, Go ye into all the world, and preach the gospel to every creature. He that believeth and is baptized shall be saved; but he that believeth not shall be damned.

And these signs shall follow them that believe; In my name shall they cast out devils; they shall speak with new tongues; They shall take up serpents; and if they drink any deadly thing, it shall not hurt them; they shall lay hands on the sick, and they shall recover."
(Mark 16:14-18)

Jesus referred to them as hard-hearted and upbraided them, yet He committed everything into their hands. He didn't wait for them to qualify for it. He believed in them.

You will never be as bad as these guys. You didn't see Jesus die on the cross and resurrect after three days. These men saw Him alive after three days yet they didn't believe.

Jesus committed His estate to you too.

The adopted son takes full charge of the estate. There are too many Christians waiting on God, but God has been waiting on them for decades. It's your move!

"For Moses describeth the righteousness which is of the

law, That the man which doeth those things shall live by them.
But the righteousness which is of faith speaketh on this wise, Say not in thine heart, Who shall ascend into heaven? (that is, to bring Christ down from above:) Or, Who shall descend into the deep? (that is, to bring up Christ again from the dead.)"
(Romans 10:5-7)

We don't have to go into heaven or into hell to try to get Jesus to help us. No!

He's delegated His authority to us.

"But as many as received him, to them gave he power (the right) to become the sons of God, even to them that believe on his name:"
(John 1:12)

We are not slaves begging God for our next meal. We are sons with the rights of sonship. It is our legal right. Use it!

Choose to prosper. Stop begging.
Choose health. Stop wishing.
Choose wisdom. Stop complaining.
Choose the good life. Stop envying.
Choose success. Stop being mediocre.
It's a choice.
It's your move!

It's all yours now—not tomorrow.

The Spirit of Adoption, the Holy Spirit, lives within you to lead you and guide you in your newfound life and status.

THE BLESSINGS OF SONSHIP

Our newfound sonship in Christ confers on us some mighty blessings, some of which I list here.

1. Fellowship

"God is faithful, by whom ye were called unto the fellowship of his Son Jesus Christ our Lord."
(1 Corinthians 1:9)

We have been called into the same fellowship that Jesus Christ has with His Father. Not a lesser degree or a different type but the same.

Prayer is now a delight. It's no more a discipline to endure.
Petition is no more a begging charade.
We have access and can fellowship with the Father—our Father.

The biggest blessing of redemption is the bestowal

of the divine nature upon a sinful man.

As birds can fellowship with birds, we as sons can now fellowship with our Father for we are carriers of His nature.

We understand Him.
We hear His voice.
We are the Church of the Firstborn, the family of the Father.

2. Inheritance

"And because ye are sons, God hath sent forth the Spirit of his Son into your hearts, crying, Abba, Father.
Wherefore thou art no more a servant, but a son; and if a son, then an heir of God through Christ."
(Galatians 4:6-7)

The inheritance we have been born into is unimaginable. The Believer in Christ is royalty. There's no reason good enough for you to fail.

There will never be a reason good enough for you to be in lack.

None whatsoever.

We are heirs of God through Jesus Christ. Our position as adopted sons frees us from the tyranny of the law and from trying to please God by works. We are the beloved in His house.

Our position as heirs and the right to the inheritance is entirely a gift from God.

"For ye have not received the spirit of bondage again to fear; but ye have received the Spirit of adoption, whereby we cry, Abba, Father.
The Spirit itself beareth witness with our spirit, that we are the children of God:
And if children, then heirs; heirs of God, and joint-heirs with Christ, if so be that we suffer with him, that we may be also glorified together."
(Romans 8:15-17a)

We are joint-heirs with Christ. We are equal inheritors with Christ in the estate of the Father.

Our minds will need a thousand years to process a tenth of what this holds for us.

We are joint-heirs, with Christ, of the wealth, power, health, wisdom, riches, anointing, honour, etc., of the Father.

Oh, the magnitude of this! Oh, that the eyes of our inner man may be flooded with light to see this.

The only clause attached is if we suffer with him. This suffering does not mean suffering as generally used. It is suffering together with Christ that is in view here.

The question then is what the suffering of Christ

was. Did He suffer from sickness or lack? No!

Heirs don't suffer from such.

The suffering here is what Christ had to endure to fulfil the will and plan of His Father here on earth.

This is the same suffering the Believer is called into today—the suffering of a bondservant. We are sons who serve the will of our Father.

3. Guidance

"For as many as are led by the Spirit of God, they are the sons of God."
(Romans 8:14)

The Holy Spirit is the Spirit of Adoption. What the law of Moses failed to do for Israel, the Holy Spirit is doing in the Believer today.

The Holy Spirit has cleansed our conscience from the condemnation and guilt that made us shrink from God in fear and has enabled the child of God to call God, Father.

He has become our guide, called alongside us, to help us walk in this new life that we have.

If we yield to Him and listen to Him, He leads us into the fullness of our inheritance in Christ.

Some try to preach that there are babies and mature sons and that the difference between them is that the Spirit leads the sons. That's far from what John was saying.

He meant that you wouldn't find a son who is not led by the Spirit.

We are sons, and the Holy Spirit is our guide.

SECTION TWO

Bondslave

"If anyone desires to be My disciple,

let him deny himself [disregard, lose sight of, and forget himself *and his own interests]*

and take up his cross and follow Me [cleave steadfastly to Me, conform wholly to

My example in living and, if need be, in dying, also]."

Jesus
The Gospel of Saint Matthew 16:24
AMPC

"None of us lives to himself [but to the Lord], and none of us dies to himself [but to the Lord, for] If we live, we live to the Lord, and if we die, we die to the Lord.

So then, whether we live or we die, we belong to the Lord.

For Christ died and lived again for this very purpose, that He might be Lord both of the dead and of the living."

Apostle Paul
The Epistle to the Romans 14:7-9
AMPC

Your Reasonable Service

"*It was just before the Passover Festival. Jesus knew that the hour had come for him to leave this world and go to the Father. Having loved his own who were in the world, he loved them to the end.*

The evening meal was in progress, and the devil had already prompted Judas, the son of Simon Iscariot, to betray Jesus.

Jesus knew that the Father had put all things under his power, and that he had come from God and was returning to God;

So he got up from the meal, took off his outer clothing, and wrapped a towel around his waist.

After that, he poured water into a basin and began to wash his disciples' feet, drying them with the towel that was wrapped around him."
(John 13:1-5 NIV)

It had been a very long day. Supper was all that was on their minds. And after that, a good night's rest, tucked in beneath the covers.

The master's itinerary had been unusually busy. It's Passover season, so most people who live far from Jerusalem are seizing the opportunity to see and hear from the miracle worker whose fame had blazed like wildfire.

The sun had set, and finally, they could head to the upper room. Lazi ly they climbed the stairs wishing it were shorter. They unbuckled their sandals by the door. Their feet bore testimony to how much work they had done in the day—dusty, dirty and smelling.

One by one, they took their seats around the table. The Master was the last to sit—at the edge of the table.

On the floor was a towel, some waterpots, a pitcher and a small basin. The custom was that one of the servants in the house would wash and massage the feet of a guest. If it is a wealthy house, a sweet-smelling ointment was applied to keep the feet supple and douse the foul smell. The lowliest of servants were responsible for this task, not just any servant—the least of the least.

After a few moments, Jesus stood up to remove His outer garment. They all assumed He wanted to be more comfortable after a long day.

Instead, He picked the servant's girdle from the wall and wrapped it around His waist.

Gently, He walked towards the waterpots. His steps were slow and frail. The Master was obviously tired and needed some rest.

He filled the pitcher with water from the waterpots, picked the basin and walked towards the disciples.

Jesus kneeled before one of the disciples, gently lifted his foot, placed it in the basin, covered it with water from the pitcher and began to wash it. When He was done with the washing, He wiped the feet with the towel around His waist.

One by one, one stinking foot after another, Jesus worked his way around the table.

Anyone who walked in at this point would have imagined that it was the lowest ranking servant that was kneeling with the towel and basin, but not in this case, this was the monarch of the universe.

It doesn't feel right to see that the very hands that formed these feet were washing them.

It doesn't feel right that the palm upon which the earth rotated would now clean away grime.

And someday soon, the one whom every knee shall bow to was kneeling before his disciples.

It feels wrong altogether.

Someone once asked, "what would you do if you knew you had just a few hours to live?" I always wondered how best to answer the question. But I found the answer in Jesus.

Hours before his death, Jesus' concern was Service!

What was His motivation? He obviously did not need to impress anyone.

Why would the creator kneel to wash the feet of the created?

He knew all things. He knew that these feet would soon desert Him.

One of the feet would soon sell Him and betray Him with a kiss—and yes, He washed those feet too!

What a solemn moment that must have been.

Many scholars have written volumes on why the Lord chose to do this. I think, for the most part, they are all right. But the text itself gives us a brilliant cue.

"Jesus knowing that the Father had given all things into his hands, and that he was come from God, and went to God;
He riseth from supper..."
(John 13:3-4)

Jesus rose from His meal to wash their feet because of a fresh awareness of His inheritance and deity.

What God had done for Him made Him serve others.

For Jesus, the greater you are, the more you need to serve.

The greatest in this kingdom are those who serve.

"But he that is greatest among you shall be your servant. And whosoever shall exalt himself shall be abased; and he that shall humble himself shall be exalted."
(Matthew 23:11-12)

MAMA ZEBEDEE...

"Hello Rabbi," she said trembling, as she knelt before Him, held on to his ankles and did obeisance. Her two sons, family men in their own right, stood, bowing slightly to courtesy the Rabbi too.

She had a seriousness in her tone. The rabbi waited on her to make her request.

"What do you want?" He asked. She reminded Him of Mary, His mother.

Her request shocked the Master. No one had ever asked such. It was a first!

"Grant that these my two sons may sit, the one on thy right hand, and the other on the left, in thy kingdom..."
(Matthew 20:21)

She wanted the best slots for her kids. She didn't care if the rest remained standing.

As expected, the other disciples were furious. They weren't just upset. The Bible says they "were moved with indignation" which is a very strong term. It indicates verbal outbursts and the possibility of physical violence.

"Who do they think they are?"

"When did they join this ministry to think they can demand such?"

"And they dare to bring their mother to beg? I thought they were adults!"

"Ridiculous! I'm disappointed with these guys. To think that we are friends!"

"Well, I'm not shocked. I always expected them to do this."

On and on they went until they were interrupted by the voice of the Rabbi calling them, after excusing Mrs Zebedee. He said,

"Ye know that the princes of the Gentiles exercise dominion over them, and they that are great exercise authority upon them.

*But it shall not be so among you: but whosoever **will be great among you, let him be your minister; And whosoever will be chief among you, let him be your servant:***

Even as the Son of man came not to be ministered unto, but to minister, and to give his life a ransom for many." (Matthew 20:25-28)

By human standards, the greatest is the one with the most regal apparel, best car, highest title and whatnot. But Jesus flipped the rules—the greatest is the one who serves.

This kingdom operates differently. We are royalty by descent but servants by choice.

Jesus came to serve and not to be served. He wasn't entitled.

CHANNELS OR CONTAINERS

Many years back, I remember coming across an interesting comparison of the water bodies in Israel.

The River Jordan connects the Sea of Galilee and the Dead Sea.

Interestingly, there's so much life around the Sea of Galilee. The area has green mountains for a landscape and several migratory birds camp there. Thousands of common cranes and pelicans flock to the area, as well as a diverse species of raptors like the eagles.

In contrast, the Dead Sea is dead! It's a lifeless body of water located in a very rugged and desolate region.

The question then is, if both seas are from the same source, why the marked difference?

The answer is simple—the water of the Sea of Galilee flows into the Dead Sea, but the Dead Sea does not give water.

The Dead Sea has no outlet to let water escape from its basin, and the only way for water to get out is by evaporation—resulting in a huge concentration of salts and other rich mineral deposits.

The water is so salty that no life, not even bacteria, can live there.

These two seas are perfect descriptions of the kinds of Believers in the Church today. Both are receiving from the same source, but one is a channel the other a container. We have received so much from God, the only way to keep it fresh and vital is to use it to serve His purposes, serve His body, the Church, and serve the good of our fellow men.

Service is probably the noblest task of the kingdom, yet many Believers grossly undermine it.

Repeatedly, Jesus made it abundantly clear that the only path to growth and promotion in the kingdom is service. I know that this is counter-culture in a world obsessed with self.

Service isn't just the fundamental principle of the kingdom. It is the fundamental principle of life. It is the only way up.

David didn't set out to kill Goliath. His father sent him to check on the welfare of his brothers and take food to them. It was while serving that an opportunity opened up for him through Goliath.

Think of it this way, the anointing on his life and the prophecies that had gone ahead of him only found expression through the channel of service.

What if David had thought that he was too big for such tasks, considering that Prophet Samuel, had singled him out from his brothers and anointed him king of Israel?

YOUR REASONABLE SERVICE

"I beseech you therefore, brethren, by the mercies of God, that ye present your bodies a living sacrifice, holy, acceptable unto God, which is your reasonable service." (Romans 12:1)

Paul's admonition here is in the light of the indescribable mercy we have received from God. If you read the preceding verses that lead into chapter twelve, you'll see that Paul was discussing the unmerited and overwhelming mercy God extended to the Gentiles. It is in view of this that he gives his counsel.

This is clearer in some more recent translations.

"Beloved friends, what should be our proper response to God's marvelous mercies? I encourage you to surrender yourselves to God to be his sacred, living sacrifices. And live in holiness, experiencing all that delights his heart. For this becomes your genuine expression of worship."
(TPT)

"I appeal to you therefore, brethren, and beg of you in view of [all] the mercies of God, to make a decisive dedication of your bodies [presenting all your members and faculties] as a living sacrifice, holy (devoted, consecrated) and well pleasing to God, which is your reasonable (rational, intelligent) service and spiritual worship."
(AMPC)

"And so, dear brothers, I plead with you to give your bodies to God. Let them be a living sacrifice, holy —the kind he can accept. **When you think of what he has done for you, is this too much to ask?"**
(TLB)

Service is a response—it is responding in gratitude to God for all He has done for you by giving yourself over to His purposes.

Paul calls it a reasonable, logical, rational response.
It's just logical to give ourselves over to serve Him in the light of the love and mercy He has showered us.

To do otherwise will be senseless!

Our reasonable service is threefold,

1. Follow the plans and purposes of God for your life.

We all have our plans and the way we want our lives to go, but God has a predetermined plan for your life.
Your job isn't to come up with a plan but to find the plan and commit to living out every single detail of that plan.
Be not wise in your own eyes. Yield and consecrate your life to Him.
His worst plan will always be far better than your best plan, and He has no worst plans.

2. Edify His Body, the Church.

You cannot serve Jesus in person. He's in heaven, but you can serve Him by serving His body.

We serve His body by winning souls, giving, intercession, volunteering, etc.

We should never be too big to serve in our Father's house. Nothing is beneath us.

The converse is that we should refrain from anything that doesn't build the Church. You can't claim to serve the Lord and tear down His bride with critical statements. That's not the Spirit of Christ.

3. Serve the good of your fellow men.

Every human is created in the image of God. We must strive to be a blessing to the world around us, particularly when they cannot serve us in return.

Bondslaves Of Love

*"The revelation of Jesus Christ, which God gave unto Him, to show unto **His servants** things which must shortly come to pass; and he sent and signified it by his angel unto his servant John:"*
(Revelation 1:1)

The scriptures were written based on the history of the ancient nation of Israel.

It is practically impossible to fully understand the context of the Bible without reading the customs and history of the nation. Such is the case with the word, 'servant'.

The idea of servants and slavery evokes unpleasant emotions in our times so much that we do not want Christianity associated with it at all.

The word 'servant' has far more implications than we know. It's a word with rich and varied applications in the Bible.

The Greek word '*doulos*', translated servant, is better-translated slave or bondslave. In Bible days, a household servant was pretty much a human chattel.

He was like a workhorse or a beast of burden, in the sense that his master owned him.

His master's will was his will, and he could not determine a destiny for himself.

'*Douloi*' were the property of their masters, and their life assignment was to obey their masters. They were devoted to their masters' interests to the extent that they disregarded their interests.

A '*doulos*' was bound to his master in a permanent relationship only death could break.

It is remarkable and very instructive to notice the frequency with which the New Testament writers used that word "bondslave" as the most appropriate term to describe their relationship to Jesus Christ!

It's actually impossible to read through the epistles without being struck by its frequency!

Quite striking for me is the Lord 's half-brothers— James and Jude. They were His siblings. They grew up in the same house and ate the same meals. Interestingly, none of His siblings believed in Him as the Messiah while He was on earth neither were they His disciples. Yet at this point, they considered it rude to be referred to as His brother. They would rather be called a bondslave.

*"James, **a servant of God and of the Lord Jesus Christ,** to the twelve tribes which are scattered abroad, greeting."*
(James 1:1)

*"Jude, **the servant of Jesus Christ, and brother of James,** to them that are sanctified by God the Father, and preserved in Jesus Christ, and called:"*
(Jude 1:1)

Do you notice that Jude introduced himself as the brother of James but not Jesus?

Their brother was now their Master, and they gladly served as His bondslaves.

Simon Peter was no different.

*"Simon Peter, **a servant and an apostle of Jesus Christ,** to them that have obtained like precious faith with us through the righteousness of God and our Saviour Jesus Christ:"*
(2 Peter 1:1)

This term was the favourite designation of the apostle, Paul, who began a couple of his epistles describing himself as a bondslave of Jesus.

"*Paul, **a servant of Jesus Christ**, called to be an apostle, separated unto the gospel of God,*"
(Romans 1:1)

This is so beautiful. Paul paints the most beautiful pictures with words. He describes himself as a servant that God called into an office- the apostolic office. The office didn't define Him. What defined him was his service. Too many ministers of the gospel today have flipped the script—they are apostles who are servants, pastors who are servants...so wrong!

Service is at the core of the kingdom of God!

"*Paul and Timotheus, the servants of Jesus Christ, to all the saints in Christ Jesus which are at Philippi, with the bishops and deacons:*"
(Philippians 1:1)

"*Paul, a servant of God, and an apostle of Jesus Christ, according to the faith of God's elect, and the acknowledging of the truth which is after godliness;*"
(Titus 1:1)

The bondslaves that John wrote the book of Revelation to are the kings and priests upon God's throne! This is the beauty of our Christian walk.

Oh, the mystery of it! Oh, the wonder of it!

He has made us kings and priests unto Him, yet we are gladly His bondslaves.

"The Revelation of Jesus Christ, which God gave unto him, to shew unto his servants things which must shortly come to pass; and he sent and signified it by his angel unto his servant John:
And from Jesus Christ, who is the faithful witness, and the first begotten of the dead, and the prince of the kings of the earth. Unto him that loved us, and washed us from our sins in his own blood, **And hath made us kings and priests unto God and his Father;** *to him be glory and dominion for ever and ever. Amen."*
(Revelation 1:1, 5-6)

THE MAKING OF A BONDSLAVE

God gave Israel much more than Ten Commandments. He gave them rules that governed business, social interactions and nation building. One of such provisions was for the Bondservant. It was so vital that a Bible scholar notes that this was the first provision God gave Israel right after giving the Ten Commandments—and He repeated it for emphasis. (Exodus 21 and Deuteronomy 15).

God made provisions that if an Israelite, through

unfavourable business, disappointing harvests or poor financial decisions, were to fall into some huge debt to a wealthy neighbour—he could deed his property over to his creditor until the year of Jubilee.

If after giving his property, the value of the debt was still much more than what he has provided, he could deliver himself to his creditor to be his servant to work off his debt.

This must have been the case of the dead prophet whose two sons were to be taken away into slavery.

"Now there cried a certain woman of the wives of the sons of the prophets unto Elisha, saying, Thy servant my husband is dead; and thou knowest that thy servant did fear the Lord: and the creditor is come to take unto him my two sons to be **bondmen.***"*
(2 Kings 4:1)

Once the man has delivered himself as a servant, he is free from anxiety and the fear of the creditor knocking on the door every year, blowing threats down his throat.

All the responsibility for food, clothing, shelter, and the welfare of the debtor and his family was now transferred to the creditor—the new master.

When the appointed years have passed and the debt satisfied, the master would call the slave to review the contract and effect his release.

But God added an incredible clause. If the man preferred to stay with his master whether because he doubted his ability to make it on his own again; or he truly loved his master; or he enjoyed the terms of service to his master; or he was pleased with the welfare he and his family enjoyed in his masters house; he had the choice to bind himself to that master's service forever! This was irrevocable.

If however, he decided to leave, he could only take with him what was his before he became a slave. Whatever his master gave him during his service years stayed behind, even a wife!

If he became a slave as a married man, his wife went with him. However, if it was his master that gave him a wife and she had given birth to sons or daughters, they could not accompany him.

"Now these are the judgments which thou shalt set before them. If thou buy an Hebrew servant, six years he shall serve: and in the seventh he shall go out free for nothing. If he came in by himself, he shall go out by himself: if he were married, then his wife shall go out with him. If his master have given him a wife, and she have born him sons or daughters; the wife and her children shall be her master's, and he shall go out by himself."
(Exodus 21:1-4)

If his master was pleased with him and desired him

to stay, the master will take the servant before the judges of the city. After which, he shall take the servant to a door or a doorframe and pierce his ear with an awl. An awl was a short sharp rod used to pierce leather. Needless to say, this was a painful ceremony! It was called the Opening of the Ear. This is very significant, as you shall soon see.

The mark created by the awl sealed his relationship to his master forever and distinguished him from everyone. At first glance, you immediately could tell that he was a bondservant.

From that moment, he was a marked man!

The ornament inserted in the hole of the ear, much like a lady's earring, bore testimony that he was the slave of another by his own choice. He wasn't a servant of compulsion or circumstance but of choice. Much more, it was a testament to his master's character that he was a good man—that his master took better care of him than he could.

You now understand the implications to the early Christians when the apostles called themselves bondservants. It was more a testimony to the character of their Lord than of themselves. Some wrote from prison, yet they wore their badges proudly. Even in prison, He was a good Lord!

The pierced ear of a bondslave implied that his lord

had his ear, which meant that he willingly chose to obey his master's voice!

This was what the prophet Isaiah declared about the coming Messiah. He came as a bondservant of the Most High.

"The Lord God hath given me the tongue of the learned, that I should know how to speak a word in season to him that is weary: **he wakeneth morning by morning,he wakeneth mine ear to hear as the learned.**
The Lord God hath **opened mine ear,** *and I was not rebellious, neither turned away back."*
(Isaiah 50:4-5)

There's another detail I want you to see,

"And if the servant shall plainly say, **I love my master,** *my wife, and my children; I will not go out free: Then his master shall bring him unto the judges; he shall also bring him to the door, or unto the door post; and his master shall bore his ear through with an awl; and he shall serve him for ever."*
(Exodus 21:5-6)

The initial contract was based on debts, but the new one was based on love. Henceforth, he no longer served his master to pay off any debt—he served him willingly out of a heart of love.

The slave is free to go, to live his own life and to be his own boss, but his master's way of life and his experience in his house influenced him so much that he was now bound to his master by something higher and stronger than the commandment that kept him. Now the slave says, "I LOVE MY MASTER! I LOVE MY MASTER'S FAMILY! I WILL NOT BE FREE! I LOVE MY MASTER MORE THAN MY FREEDOM!"

This had to be the result of genuine love for his master, not duty or obligation or favours or benefits.

From the day he decided to give himself to his master, in love and service for forever, he stopped being a mere slave—he became a bondslave, a love-slave!

"For the love of Christ constraineth us;..."
(2 Corinthians 5:14)

In life and death, he was bound to his master. He didn't feel that his life was too much to give to his master.

Little wonder Paul said,

"None of us lives to himself [but to the Lord], and none of us dies to himself [but to the Lord, for]
If we live, we live to the Lord, and if we die, we die to the Lord . So then, whether we live or we die, we belong to the

Lord.
For Christ died and lived again for this very purpose, that
He might be Lord both of the dead and of the living."
(Romans 14:7-9)

Being a bondslave was so real to the early Church
that practically all the early apostles and fathers died
as martyrs for the faith they professed. They loved not
their lives unto the death.

What mattered most was what pleased their new
Lord.

Love was their Lord. Love was their motivation.

We must be willing to give up all our rights. As
bondslaves of love, we must be willing and ready to be
subject to Jesus as absolute Lord and King of our lives!

We find, then, that God has called us out of bondage
and into bondage!

We realise that the zenith of freedom is service to
our Lord.

Such is the love that we have found that we would
deliberately choose bondage rather than liberty.

And here's the irony—the one who is bound to the
Lord is the free man, and the one who is loosed from
him is most bound.

A son is what **the Father makes us**! Sonship is the
work of God! We did not call ourselves to sonship!

On the other hand, a bondslave is what **we make ourselves!** It is our choice.

Paul, The Pattern Servant

"This is a faithful saying, and worthy of all acceptation, that Christ Jesus came into the world to save sinners; of whom I am chief.
Howbeit for this cause I obtained mercy, that in me first Jesus Christ might shew forth all longsuffering, for a pattern to them which should hereafter believe on him to life everlasting."
(1 Timothy 1:15-16)

Paul wrote to his protégé, a younger and less experienced Timothy, advising him about the work of the ministry.

The Apostle was very clear about the call on his life. He knew God's assignment for his life and in these verses is one part of his call that we easily miss out.

He stated why He obtained mercy in Jesus. His life

was simply an example of what God can do with the vilest sinner.

I, however, believe that there's another layer of truth to this—Paul's life was to be a pattern of what God expects of the Believer and what our lives can become when yielded to the mercy of Jesus.

Paul was the pattern servant—the pattern bondslave. With his life, he gives us an example of what our consecration to God's plans for our lives should look like and ultimately, our commitment to the gospel.

Paul, in no way, takes the place of our Lord Jesus. Jesus remains our perfect example, but Jesus singled Paul out to show us a pattern we can emulate.

Sprinkled throughout the New Testament are lessons from the life of Paul. I have summarised them into these:

1. The Humility of A Bondslave
2. Pleasing the Master—the one desire of a Bondslave
3. The Marks of Christ, A Bondslaves' Stars
4. The Master's will is law, not a suggestion
5. Eternity in View, not temporal gains

1. The Humility of A Bondslave

Paul was not a man of mean intelligence. His pedigree made even the most educated feel inferior. Until Paul, it seemed that Christians were a bunch of uneducated fellows who were occupied with the newest fad. But Paul's entrance into the picture changed it all. He wasn't Peter, the fisherman. This was Paul who described himself like this:

"I am a Jew, born in Tarsus in Cilicia, but brought up in this city, educated at the feet of Gamaliel according to the strict manner of the law of our fathers, being zealous for God as all of you are this day."
(Acts 22:3)

He trained to be a lawyer under the best, Gamaliel. Gamaliel sat on the council of the Sanhedrin, and one time, the Bible records that when they had to make a decision, Gamaliel's counsel was followed. (Acts 5:34-39)

He was considered one of the wisest men of that time.

Paul had dual nationality; he could claim Jewish heritage and claim to be Roman. He was a well-respected figure in the society, one who used his position and means to persecute and decimate the Church. Remember he was the one who oversaw the stoning of Stephen.

Paul's zeal was second to none. He described it in Galatians 1:14 as "*advancing in Judaism beyond many of my own age among my people, so extremely zealous was I for the traditions of my fathers*".

In Philippians, Paul pulls no stops when rolling out his impressive pedigree,

"*Though I might also have confidence in the flesh. **If any other man thinketh that he hath whereof he might trust in the flesh, I more**: Circumcised the eighth day, of the stock of Israel, of the tribe of Benjamin, an Hebrew of the Hebrews; as touching the law, a Pharisee; Concerning zeal, persecuting the Church; touching the righteousness which is in the law, blameless.*"
(Philippians 3:4-6)

He had the MBAs, PhDs and all the degrees you could imagine. Impressive, I must say.
Paul was the top dog. He had justifiable reasons to be a proud man.

But after his encounter with the Lord, he says,

"***But what things were gain to me, those I counted loss for Christ.** Yea doubtless, and I count all things but loss for the excellency of the knowledge of Christ Jesus my*

Lord: for whom I have suffered the loss of all things, and **do count them but dung,** *that I may win Christ,"* (Philippians 3:7-8)

Paul flushes it all down the drain. These things that are gains to the world are now dung to him. What the world glories in doesn't concern a bondslave.

The world glories in qualifications, accomplishments, accumulations and positions, but they are all dung to the bondslave of Christ. His self-worth and value doesn't come from this.

Our highest honour is to serve Jesus. There's no higher honour in all the universe. None!

Several Believers think certain tasks are beneath them. When God blesses them, they consider it belittling for someone of their stature to engage in some chores in the house of God. Quite unfortunate!

David was anointed king of the whole Israel, but he said, *"For a day in thy courts is better than a thousand. I had rather be a doorkeeper in the house of my God, than to dwell in the tents of wickedness."* (Psalm 84:10)

Little wonder God called him a man after His heart.

Bondservants burn the flesh. They put all trophies

aside, fold their sleeves and serve their Lord with all humility.

And whatever He demands is never too dishonouring for them regardless of their stature.

Have you counted it all loss just to gain Christ?

The other dimension to this is following God at all costs. Given what He has done for us, there's nothing too great to give up for him.

Many people considered me a fool for giving up the job and financial security medical training provides for the uncertainty of ministry.

While in high school, my friend and I had the best grades. He's a preacher too today. One of my teachers saw me and lamented, "What a waste?!" He was unhappy that his brightest brains were now pastors. We should have pursued a secular career he said. I laughed and asked him, "So Jesus should get the dullards?"

That is not to say that it is wrong to pursue a secular career. Why not, if that's God's plan for your life?

2. Pleasing the Master—the one desire of a Bondslave

"No man that warreth entangleth himself with the affairs

of this life; **that he may please him who hath chosen him to be a soldier."**
(2 Timothy 2:4)

"For every soldier called to active duty must divorce himself from the distractions of this world **so that he may fully satisfy the one who chose him."**
(TPT)

"and as Christ's soldier, do not let yourself become tied up in worldly affairs, **for then you cannot satisfy the one who has enlisted you in his army."**
(TLB)

A bondservant has only one desire; to please his master.

Many things are lawful and right, but not all things are expedient. You must live your life in consideration of the hand of the Lord on you.

Many people have been sidetracked from following God's plan for their lives simply because they are too concerned with what people will say or think of them.

The obsession with people's approval is one of the biggest reasons for missing God's will. And as long as you are concerned about approval ratings, you can never truly be the Lord's bondslave.

Seeking people's approval or validation is an

addiction—break away from it. You are approved in Christ! That's all that matters.

"For do I now persuade men, or God? or do I seek to please men? for if I yet pleased men, I should not be the servant of Christ."
(Galatians 1:10)

He whose focus is to please men cannot be the servant of Christ.

3. The Marks of Christ, A Bondslaves' Stars

"But the Lord said unto him, Go thy way: for he is a chosen vessel unto me, to bear my name before the Gentiles, and kings, and the children of Israel:
For I will shew him how great things he must suffer for my name's sake."
(Acts 9:15-16)

Following God is hard on the flesh—being a bondslave isn't easy on the flesh.

Many times the flesh wants its way and its plans, but a bondslave has given up the right to his life for his Lord and Master.

We, Believers, don't like to talk about suffering but it's part of the package. This has nothing to do with sicknesses and poverty. These are hardships and sufferings we experience as we follow our master— they are the cross we have to bear.

Paul admonished Timothy, "*Thou therefore endure hardness, as a good soldier of Jesus Christ.*" (2 Timothy 2:3)

A good soldier of Jesus endures hardness. Too many people want to follow at their convenience. You can't decide the rules of engagement. The master does.

Prayer is hard on the flesh.

Giving sacrificially is hard on the flesh.

Persecution is hard on the flesh.

Walking in love and not retaliating is hard on the flesh.

The sacrifices we make to pursue the call on our lives aren't always easy. They could be very tough!

But in the light of what He has done for us, they are not that big enough to be truly called sacrifices.

And like Brother Hagin will always say, "payday doesn't come every Saturday night. But it surely comes!"

Paul puts it this way, "*For God is not unrighteous to forget your work and labour of love, which ye have shewed toward his name.*" (Hebrews 6:10)

Remember the impressive credentials Paul counts as dung in Philippians 3? Look at his new credentials, what he now glories in:

"Are they ministers of Christ? (I speak as a fool) I am more; in labours more abundant, in stripes above measure, in prisons more frequent, in deaths oft.

Of the Jews five times received I forty stripes save one.

Thrice was I beaten with rods, once was I stoned, thrice I suffered shipwreck, a night and a day I have been in the deep;

In journeyings often, in perils of waters, in perils of robbers, in perils by mine own countrymen, in perils by the heathen, in perils in the city, in perils in the wilderness, in perils in the sea, in perils among false brethren;

In weariness and painfulness, in watchings often, in hunger and thirst, in fastings often, in cold and nakedness.

Beside those things that are without, that which cometh upon me daily, the care of all the Churches.

Who is weak, and I am not weak? Who is offended, and I burn not?

If I must needs glory, I will glory of the things which concern mine infirmities.

The God and Father of our Lord Jesus Christ, which is blessed for evermore, knoweth that I lie not.

In Damascus the governor under Aretas the king kept the city of the Damascenes with a garrison, desirous to

apprehend me:
And through a window in a basket was I let down by the
wall, and escaped his hands."
(2 Corinthians 11:23-33)

These were his scars, but he considered them
badges for the kingdom.
No one truly serves without scars.
He called them the marks of the Lord Jesus.

"But God forbid that I should glory, save in the cross of
our Lord Jesus Christ, by whom the world is crucified unto
me, and I unto the world. For in Christ Jesus neither
circumcision availeth any thing, nor uncircumcision, but
a new creature.
From henceforth let no man trouble me: ***for I bear in my***
body the marks of the Lord Jesus."
(Galatians 6:14-15, 17)

What a man!
What a pattern!
What an example!

4. The Master's will is law, not a suggestion

"And now, behold, ***I go bound in the spirit*** *unto*
Jerusalem, not knowing the things that shall befall me
there:

Save that the Holy Ghost witnesseth in every city, saying that bonds and afflictions abide me.
But none of these things move me, neither count I my life dear unto myself, so that I might finish my course with joy, and the ministry, which I have received of the Lord Jesus, to testify the gospel of the grace of God."
(Acts 20:22-24)

"I go bound in the spirit.."

The force of those words! The leading of the Spirit wasn't a suggestion to this man. He was compelled to obey. Paul was certainly bondslave.

*"And now **I am captive to the Holy Spirit** to go to Jerusalem, without really knowing what will happen to me there."*
(Acts 20:22 TPT)

One Bible footnote reads, "shackled by the Holy Spirit."

What makes this a compelling narrative is the fact that he had no idea what the future held for him on this journey except that bonds and afflictions were awaiting him. Yet he was bound by the dictates of the Spirit and did not try to negotiate his way out.

Paul's life did not matter to him. He only wanted to

follow and ultimately fulfil the plan of God for his life.

"Save that the Holy Ghost witnesseth in every city, saying that bonds and afflictions abide me.
But none of these things move me, neither count I my life dear unto myself, so that I might finish my course with joy, and the ministry, which I have received of the Lord Jesus, to testify the gospel of the grace of God."
(Acts 20:23-24)

Too many Christians are caught up with the mundane issues of life. We want a good life, a car, a house, a lot of money, etc. There's absolutely nothing wrong with all of that, but we have a higher calling. There's a divine plan hanging over your life.

His will and His plan must become law in your life.

5. Eternity in View, not temporal gains

"For I am now ready to be offered, and the time of my departure is at hand. I have fought a good fight, I have finished my course, I have kept the faith: Henceforth there is laid up for me a crown of righteousness, which the Lord, the righteous judge, shall give me at that day: and not to me only, but unto all them also that love his appearing."
(2 Timothy 4:6-8)

The ultimate goal for a bondslave is to hear "well done, thou good and faithful servant."

This is what distinguishes true servants and hirelings, bondslaves and mercenaries.

The former have their eyes fixed on eternity, and the latter on temporal gains. And once the temporal gains aren't there, they get offended in God.

Who are you?
A bondslave or a mercenary?

What's Next, Papa?

When we hear and believe the message of the Gospel, we are born out of spiritual death and awakened to the Fatherhood of God.

We are cut off from the tyranny of sin and dictatorship of satan into the liberty of the sons of God.

On the cross with Jesus, we were crucified to the world and the world to us. The world holds no attraction for us anymore.

Christianity is NOT a religion. It's a Family.

Laws bind people that practice religion. The code of our family is love.

We are the offspring of Love.

It is only a person that has truly experienced the

Love of the Father in the secret that can exercise the Power of God in public.

Faith grows out of Love.
Fellowship is the mother of faith.
Faith is not a struggle. It shouldn't be.
For the most part, faith ought to be an unconscious reality for the Believer.

There's not one record of Jesus trying to walk in faith, as we know it, neither did the apostles. None! They just walked in faith.
As we fellowship with Perfect Love through the Word and in prayer, all fear and doubts are cast out. Our faith is supercharged.

This faith is bold.
We having the same spirit of faith boldly declare. That spirit is an attitude. This faith has an attitude.
It's pioneering in nature, always peeping through the curtains asking, 'what's next to conquer?'
This faith blazes the trails of revelations, accomplishments and power.

No wonder the Apostle Paul said,

"So don't you see that we don't owe this old do-it-yourself life one red cent.
There's nothing in it for us, nothing at all. The best thing

to do is give it a decent burial and get on with your new life.

God's Spirit beckons. There are things to do and places to go! This resurrection life you received from God is not a timid, grave-tending life. It's adventurously expectant, greeting God with a childlike "What's next, Papa?"

God's Spirit touches our spirits and confirms who we really are. We know who he is, and we know who we are: Father and children.

And we know we are going to get what's coming to us - an unbelievable inheritance! We go through exactly what Christ goes through. If we go through the hard times with him, then we're certainly going to go through the good times with him!"
Romans 8:12-16 (MSG)

We have the boldness to take the world because we are one with the one who created it.

We are sons of the monarch of the universe. We are joint-heirs with Jesus.

He has committed the running of His estate to us.

As we contemplate the immense and unimaginable trust of the Father in us that he committed everything to us, we are overwhelmed in awe. In response, we scream, **"What's Next, Papa?"**

Prayer For Salvation And Baptism In The Holy Spirit

Heavenly Father, I come to You in the Name of Your Son Jesus. Your Word says, *"Whosoever shall call on the name of the Lord shall be saved"* (Acts 2:21).

I am calling on You. I pray and ask Jesus to come into my heart and be Lord over my life according to Romans 10:9-10: *"If thou shalt confess with thy mouth the Lord Jesus, and shalt believe in thine heart that God hath raised him from the dead, thou shalt be saved. For with the heart man believeth unto righteousness; and with the mouth confession is made unto salvation."*

I declare that Jesus is Lord, and I believe in my heart that God raised Him from the dead. I am now reborn! I am a child of the Almighty God! I am saved!

You also said in Your Word, *"If ye then, being evil, know how to give good gifts unto your children: HOW MUCH MORE shall your heavenly Father give the Holy Spirit to them that ask him?"* (Luke 11:13).

I, therefore, ask You to fill me with the Holy Spirit. Holy Spirit rise up within me as I praise God. I fully expect to speak with other tongues as You give me the utterance (Acts 2:4). In Jesus' Name. Amen!"

Begin to praise God for filling you with the Holy Spirit. Speak those words and syllables you receive—not in your own language, but the language given to you by the Holy Spirit. You have to use your voice. God will not force you to speak. Don't be concerned about how it sounds. It is a heavenly language! (1 Corinthians 14:2, 14).

Continue with the blessing God has given you and pray in the spirit every day. You are a born-again, Spirit-filled Believer. You'll never be the same!

Christians are like coals of fire; together they glow, but apart they grow cold. We urge you to become part of our Church family, where we will love and care for you. The Church of Jesus is a place to belong and not just something to believe. Get messages that will help you grow to be just like Jesus on our store
www.tribepetra.store
or watch our videos on our YouTube page, Petra Christian Centre.

About The Author

Ayo Ajani is the Founder and President of Tribe Petra Ministries, and Senior Pastor of Petra Christian Centre Churches, globally - a fast-growing Church ministry with centres in Lekki, Ikeja and Abuja.

His teaching and healing ministries, spanning over two decades, have impacted thousands of lives around the globe. He is graced with a unique ability to communicate God's Word in a simple, practical, yet powerful way.

Pastor Ayo is the Convener of city-wide meetings such as Prayer Seminars, Rain Conference, The Festival, and The Festival Convention, where the Word of God is taught, and an atmosphere is created for the demonstration of the gifts of the Holy Spirit.

These meetings have witnessed thousands gathered at various times, numerous bodily healing and multiple salvations recorded.

He has written several titles, amongst which are The Spiritual Freshman, Getting Acquainted with the Spirit, and Fight.

He is the host of a TV programme, *'Simply Put'*,

where he shares Spiritual Truths and Principles and how they can be applied in Believers' lives. The program, at a time, aired on Kingdom Africa.

He is also the President of Petra Leadership College, a ministry training outfit set up to equip and resource the body of Christ.

He is happily married to his wife, and best friend, Adeola Ajani and they have three children (Ayomikun, Ayomiposi & Fikayomi).

Made in the USA
Lexington, KY
25 November 2019